D0397998

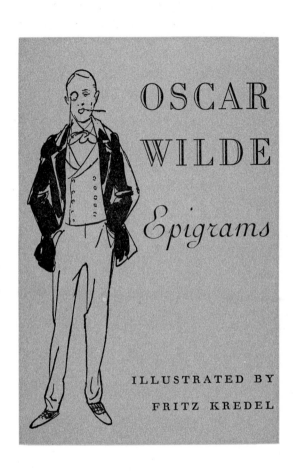

OSCAR WILDE

Epigrams

ILLUSTRATED BY

FRITZ KREDEL

THE PETER PAUPER PRESS

MOUNT VERNON • NEW YORK

Oscar Wilde · Epigrams

FROM *The Importance of Being Earnest*

BY PERSISTENTLY remaining single a man converts himself into a permanent public temptation.

Divorces are made in heaven.

One must be serious about something if one wants to have any amusement in life.

An engagement is hardly a serious one that has not been broken off at least once.

The only way to atone for being occasionally over-dressed is by being always absolutely over-educated.

One's duty as a gentleman should never interfere with one's pleasure in the slightest degree.

The truth is rarely pure and never simple. Modern life would be very tedious if it were either, and modern literature an impossibility.

The amount of women who flirt with their own husbands is scandalous. It is simply washing one's clean linen in public.

The modern sympathy with invalids is morbid. Illness of any kind is hardly a thing to be encouraged in others.

A man who desires to get married should know either everything or nothing.

The two weak points of our age are want of principle and want of profile.

Style depends largely on the way the chin is worn. They are worn very high at present.

The way to behave to a woman is to make love to her if she is pretty, and to some one else if she is plain.

Women only call each other sister after they have called each other a lot of other things first.

Memory is the diary that chronicles things that never have happened and couldn't possibly have happened.

The good end happily, the bad unhappily. That is what fiction means.

Few parents nowadays pay any regard to what their children say to them. The old-fashioned respect for the young is fast dying out.

Relations are simply a tedious pack of people who haven't got the remotest knowledge of how to live, nor the smallest instinct about when to die.

Arguments are to be avoided; they are always vulgar and often convincing.

Long engagements give people the opportunity of finding out each other's character before marriage, which is never advisable.

No woman should ever be quite accurate about her age. It looks so calculating.

Never speak disrespectfully of society. Only people who can't get into it do that.

All women become like their mothers — that is their tragedy. No man does. That's his.

Three addresses always inspire confidence — even in tradesmen.

In married life three is company and two is none.

It is important not to keep a business engagement if one wants to retain any sense of the beauty of life.

If one plays good music people don't listen, and if one plays bad music people don't talk.

What with the duties expected of one during one's lifetime, and the duties exacted from one after one's death, land has ceased to be either a profit or pleasure. It gives one position and prevents one from keeping it up.

Whenever one has anything unpleasant to say one should always be quite candid.

Flowers are as common in the country as people are in London.

It is very vulgar to talk about one's own business. Only people like stock-brokers do that, and then merely at dinner parties.

Girls never marry the men they flirt with. Girls don't think it right.

FROM *Lady Windemere's Fan*

THERE is nothing in the world like the devotion of a married woman. It is a thing no married man knows anything about.

We are all of us so hard-up nowadays that the only pleasant things to pay are compliments. They're the only things we *can* pay.

If you pretend to be good, the world takes you very seriously. If you pretend to be bad, it doesn't. Such is the astounding stupidity of optimism.

I can resist everything except temptation.

It is a curious thing about the game of marriage — a game, by the way, that is going out of fashion — the wives hold all the honors and invariably lose the odd trick.

A heart doesn't go with modern dress. It makes one look old.

Nowadays to be intelligible is to be found out.

Nothing looks so like innocence as an indiscretion.

A cynic is a man who knows the price of everything, and the value of nothing.

A sentimentalist is a man who sees an absurd value in everything and doesn't know the market price of a single thing.

The world is packed with good women. To know them is a middle-class education.

Life is far too important a thing ever to talk seriously about.

What consoles one nowadays is not repentance, but pleasure. Repentance is quite out of date, and besides, if a woman really repents, she has to go to a bad dressmaker, otherwise no one believes in her.

My own business always bores me to death. I prefer other people's.

Wicked women bother one, good women bore one. That is the only difference between them.

Women always want one to be good. And if we are good when they meet us, they don't love us at all. They like to find us quite irretrievably bad and to leave us quite unattractively good.

A mother who doesn't part with a daughter every season has no real affection.

The world has grown suspicious of anything that looks like a happy married life.

It is most dangerous nowadays for a husband to pay any attention to his wife in public. It always makes people think that he beats her when they are alone.

Nature's gentlemen are the worst type of gentlemen I know.

Even business should have a picturesque background. With a proper background a woman can do anything.

When men give up saying what is charming, they cease thinking what is charming.

It is an awfully dangerous thing to come across a woman who thoroughly understands one. They always end by marrying one.

One can always recognize women who trust their husbands, they look so thoroughly unhappy.

Crying is the refuge of plain women but the ruin of pretty ones.

Men are such cowards. They outrage every law of the world, and are afraid of the world's tongue.

How marriage ruins a man! It is as demoralizing as cigarettes, and far more expensive.

The youth of the present day are quite monstrous. They have absolutely no respect for dyed hair.

Ideals are dangerous things. Realities wound, but they are better.

Misfortunes one can endure — they come from outside, they are accidents. But to suffer for one's own faults — Ah! there is the sting of life.

It takes a thoroughly good woman to do a thoroughly stupid thing.

Good people do a great deal of harm in the world. Certainly the greatest harm they do is that they make badness of such extraordinary importance. It is absurd to divide people into good and bad. People are either charming or tedious.

Men may become old, but they never become good.

My experience is that as soon as people are old enough to know better, they don't know anything at all.

Actions are the first tragedies in life, words are the second. Words are perhaps the worst. Words are merciless.

We are all in the gutter, but some of us are looking at the stars.

In this world there are only two tragedies. One is not getting what one wants, and the other is getting it. The last is much the worst; the last is a real tragedy!

FROM *An Ideal Husband*

FASHION is what one wears oneself. What is unfashionable is what other people wear.

Morality is simply the attitude we adopt toward people whom we personally dislike.

Musical people are so absurdly unreasonable. They always want one to be perfectly dumb at the very moment when one is longing to be absolutely deaf.

Nothing is so dangerous as being too modern; one is apt to grow old-fashioned quite suddenly.

Nothing ages women so rapidly as having married the general rule.

Vulgarity is simply the conduct of other people, just as falsehoods are the truths of other people.

Being educated puts one almost on a level with the commercial classes.

If one could only teach the English how to talk and the Irish how to listen society would be quite civilized.

London society is entirely composed of beautiful idiots and brilliant lunatics.

Political parties are the only places left to us where people don't talk politics.

A man who allows himself to be convinced by an argument is a thoroughly unreasonable person, which accounts for so much in women that their husbands never appreciate in them.

Only dull people are brilliant at breakfast.

In modern life nothing produces such an effect as a good platitude. It makes the whole world kin.

Secrets from other people's wives are a necessary luxury in modern life, but no man should have a secret from his own wife. She invariably finds out. Women have a wonderful instinct about things. They can discover everything except the obvious.

There is only one real tragedy in a woman's life. The fact that her past is always her lover, and her future invariably her husband.

No woman, plain or pretty, has any common-sense at all. Common-sense is the privilege of our sex and we men are so self-sacrificing that we never use it.

Spies are of no use nowadays. Their profession is over. The newspapers do their work instead.

One should always play fairly when one has the winning cards.

An acquaintance that begins with a compliment is sure to develop into a real friendship.

Optimism begins in a broad grin, and Pessimism ends with blue spectacles. Both are merely poses.

Romance should never begin with sentiment. It should begin with science and end with a settlement.

In the case of a very fascinating woman, sex is a challenge, not a defense.

To love oneself is the beginning of a lifelong romance.

The London season is entirely matrimonial. People are either hunting for husbands or hiding from them.

Modern women find a new scandal as becoming as a new bonnet, and air them both in the Park every afternoon.

Pleasure is the only thing to live for. Nothing ages like happiness.

A woman whose size in gloves is seven and three quarters never knows much about anything.

Fathers should be neither seen nor heard. That is the only proper basis for family life.

The only thing to do with good advice is to pass it on. It is never of any use to oneself.

Philanthropy is the refuge of people who wish to annoy their fellow-creatures.

When a man has once loved a woman he will do anything for her except continue to love her.

Self-sacrifice is a thing that should be put down by law. It is so demoralizing to the people for whom one sacrifices oneself.

Pluck is not so common nowadays as genius.

Questions are never indiscreet, answers sometimes are.

Woman's first duty in life is to her dressmaker. What the second duty is no one has yet discovered.

It is always nice to be expected and not to arrive.

The reason we are so pleased to find out other people's secrets is that it distracts public attention from our own.

Women are never disarmed by compliments, men always are.

Modern women understand everything except their husbands.

The only possible society is oneself.

FROM *A Woman of No Importance*

PLAIN women are always jealous of their husbands, beautiful women never are; they have no time, they are always so occupied in being jealous of other people's husbands.

Twenty years of romance make a woman look like a ruin, but twenty years of marriage make her something like a public building.

To have the reputation of possessing the most perfect social tact, talk to every woman as if you loved her, and to every man as if he bored you.

The Soul is born old, but it grows young; that is the comedy of life. The Body is born young and grows old; that is life's tragedy.

Women are pictures, men are problems: if you want to know what a woman really means, look at her, don't listen to her.

There is no such thing as romance in our day, women have become too brilliant; nothing spoils a romance so much as a sense of humor in the woman.

One can survive everything except Death, and live down everything except a good reputation.

Simple pleasures are the last refuge of the complex.

Discontent is the first step in the progress of a man or a nation.

Sentiment is all very well for a boutonnière, but a well-tied tie is the first serious step in life.

Clever people never listen and stupid people never talk.

The youth of America is their oldest tradition. It has been going on now for three hundred years. To hear them talk one would imagine they were in their first childhood. As far as civilization goes they are in their second.

Nowadays it is only the unreadable that occurs.

Women have become so highly educated that nothing should surprise them except happy marriages.

Women as a sex are Sphinxes without secrets.

Health — the silliest word in our language — and one knows the popular idea of health. The English country gentleman galloping after a fox — the unspeakable in full pursuit of the uneatable.

It is safer to believe evil of everyone until people are found out to be good, but that requires a great deal of investigation nowadays.

The basis of every scandal is an absolutely immoral certainty.

A bad man is the sort of man who admires innocence.

To get into the best society nowadays, one has either to feed people, amuse people, or shock people.

Men always want to be a woman's first love — women like to be a man's last romance.

Children begin by loving their parents; after a time they judge them; rarely, if ever, do they forgive them.

To elope is cowardly; it is running away from danger; and danger has become so rare in modern life.

The one advantage of playing with fire is that one never even gets singed. It is the people who don't know how to play with it that get burned up.

There is no objection to plain women being Puritans; it is the only excuse they have for being plain.

A bad woman is the sort of woman a man never gets tired of.

Vulgar habit people have nowadays of asking one, after one has given them an idea, whether one is serious or not. Nothing is serious except passion. The intellect is an instrument on which one plays, that is all. The only serious form of intellect is the British intellect. And on the British form of intellect the illiterates play the drum.

We are born in an age when only the dull are treated seriously.

It is absurd to say that there are neither ruins nor curiosities in America when they have their mothers and their manners.

America is a Paradise for women — that is why, like Eve, the American women are extremely anxious to get out of it.

To give an accurate description of what has never occurred is the inalienable privilege and proper occupation of the historian.

All men are married women's property; that is the only true definition of what married women's property really is.

Society is a necessary thing. No man has any real success in this world unless he has women to back him, and women rule society. If you have not got women on your side you are quite over. You might as well be a barrister, or a stock-broker, or a journalist at once.

All Americans dress well — they get their clothes in Paris.

Women are a fascinatingly willful set. Every woman is a rebel and usually in wild revolt against herself.

The history of woman is the history of the worst form of tyranny the world has ever known: the tyranny of the weak over the strong. It is the only tyranny that lasts.

One should sympathize with the joy, the beauty, the color of life — the less said about life's sores the better.

Women have always been picturesque protests against the mere existence of common sense.

When good Americans die they go to Paris, when bad Americans die they go to America.

It is perfectly monstrous the way people go about nowadays saying things against one, behind one's back, that are absolutely and entirely true.

If a man is a gentleman he knows quite enough, and if he is not a gentleman whatever he knows is bad for him.

Duty is what one expects from others — it is not what one does oneself.

English women conceal their feelings until after they are married, then they show them.

One should never trust a woman who tells one her real age. A woman who would tell that would tell anything.

One should never take sides in anything — taking sides is the beginning of sincerity, and earnestness follows shortly after, and the human being becomes a bore.

The happiness of a married man depends on the people he has not married.

One should always be in love: that is the reason one should never marry.

The secret of life is to appreciate the pleasure of being terribly deceived.

When a man says he has exhausted life one always knows life has exhausted him.

Men know life too early, women know life too late.

The world is divided into two classes, those who believe the incredible, and those who do the improbable.

All thought is immoral. Its very essence is destruction. If you think of anything you kill it. Nothing survives being thought of.

Women have a much better time than men in this world; there are far more things forbidden to them.

To be in society is merely a bore, but to be out of it simply a tragedy.

Moderation is a fatal thing; nothing succeeds like excess.

Men are horribly tedious when they are good husbands, and abominably conceited when they are not.

American women are wonderfully clever in concealing their parents.

A really *grande passion* is comparatively rare nowadays. It is the privilege of people who have nothing to do. That is the only use of the idle classes in the country.

More marriages are ruined nowadays by the common sense of the husband than by anything else. How can a woman be expected to be happy with a man who insists on treating her as if she were a perfectly rational being?

When a man is old enough to do wrong he should be old enough to do right also.

The only difference between a saint and a sinner is that every saint has a past, and every sinner has a future.

Women love men for their defects. If men have enough of them women will forgive them everything, even their gigantic intellects.

Life is a *mauvais quart d'heure* made up of exquisite moments.

The world has always laughed at its own tragedies, that being the only way in which it has been able to bear them; consequently, whatever the world has treated seriously belongs to the comedy side of things.

A husband is a sort of promissory note — a woman is tired of meeting him.

When one has never heard a man's name in the course of one's life it speaks volumes for him; he must be quite respectable.

After a good dinner one could forgive anybody, even one's own relations.

Anybody can write a three-volume novel. It merely requires a complete ignorance of both life and literature.

Memory in a woman is the beginning of dowdiness.

FROM *The Picture of Dorian Gray*

WITH an evening coat and a white tie, even a stock broker can gain a reputation for being civilized.

One can always be kind to people one cares nothing about.

Men marry because they are tired, women because they are curious; both are disappointed.

Conscience and cowardice are really the same things. Conscience is the trade-name of the firm.

Laughter is not a bad beginning for a friendship, and it is the best ending for one.

I choose my friends for their good looks, my acquaintances for their characters, and my enemies for their brains.

The value of an idea has nothing whatever to do with the sincerity of the man who expresses it.

It is only the intellectually lost who ever argue.

We live in an age when only unnecessary things are absolutely necessary to us.

Experience is of no ethical value, it is simply the name we give our mistakes. It demonstrates that the future will be the same as the past.

Anybody can be good in the country. There are no temptations there. That is the reason why people who live out of town are so uncivilized. There are only two ways of becoming civilized. One is by being cultured, the other is by being corrupt. Country people have no opportunity of being either, so they stagnate.

The fatality of good resolutions is that they are always too late.

One should never make one's début with a scandal; one should reserve that to give interest to one's old age.

Insincerity is merely a method by which we can multiply our personalities.

To become the spectator of one's own life is to escape the suffering of life.

People who love once in their lives are really shallow people. What they call their loyalty and their fidelity is either the lethargy of custom or lack of imagination. Faithfulness is to the emotional life what constancy is to the intellectual life, simply a confession of failure.

Poets know how useful passion is for publication. Nowadays a broken heart will run to many editions.

Genius lasts longer than Beauty. That accounts for the fact that we all take such pains to over-educate ourselves.

Civilized society feels that manners are of more importance than morals, and the highest respectability is of less value than the possession of a good chef. Even the cardinal virtues cannot atone for cold entrées, nor an irreproachable private life for a bad dinner and poor wines.

Fashion is that by which the fantastic becomes for a moment universal.

Real beauty ends where an intellectual expression begins. Intellect is in itself an exaggeration and destroys the harmony of any face. The moment one sits down to think one becomes all nose or all forehead, or something horrid.

Being natural is simply a pose.

A man cannot be too careful in the choice of his enemies.

I can't help detesting my relations. I suppose it comes from the fact that we can't stand other people having the same faults as ourselves.

Women have no appreciation of good looks. At least, good women have not.

There is no such thing as good influence. All influence is immoral — immoral from the scientific point of view.

The only way a woman can ever reform a man is by boring him so completely that he loses all possible interest in life.

The reason we all like to think so well of others is that we are all afraid of ourselves. The basis of optimism is sheer terror.

A cigarette is the perfect type of pleasure; it is exquisite and leaves one unsatisfied.

There are only two kinds of people who are really fascinating: people who know everything, and people who know nothing.

The secret of remaining young is never to have an emotion that is unbecoming.

There is always something ridiculous about the passions of people whom one has ceased to love.

Nothing can cure the soul but the senses, just as nothing can cure the senses but the soul.

Whenever a man does a thoroughly stupid thing it is always from the noblest motive.

There is only one thing in the world worse than being talked about, and that is not being talked about.

Young men want to be faithful and are not, old men want to be faithless and cannot.

There is luxury in self-reproach. When we blame ourselves we feel no one else has a right to blame us.

The worst of having a romance is that it leaves one so unromantic.

When a woman finds out that her husband is absolutely indifferent to her she either becomes dreadfully dowdy or wears very smart bonnets that some other woman's husband has to pay for.

Beauty is a form of Genius — is higher indeed, than Genius, as it needs no explanation. People say sometimes that Beauty is only superficial, but at least it is not so superficial as thought. It is only shallow people who do not judge by appearances.

We live in an age that reads too much to be wise and thinks too much to be beautiful.

Punctuality is the thief of time.

Nothing makes one so vain as being told that one is a sinner.

In good society, taking some one's else admirer when one loses one's own always whitewashes a woman.

Good resolutions are a useless attempt to interfere with scientific laws; their origin pure vanity, their results absolutely nil.

One should absorb the color of life, but one should never remember its details.

The charm of the past is that it is past, but women never know when the curtain has fallen. They always want a sixth act.

The only difference between a caprice and a lifelong passion is that a caprice lasts a little longer.

Death and vulgarity are the only two facts in the nineteenth century that one cannot explain away.

I like Wagner's music better than any other music. It is so loud that one can talk the whole time without people hearing what one says. That is a great advantage.

One can never pay too high a price for any sensation.

To test the Reality we must see it on the tight rope. When the verities become acrobats we can judge them.

I can stand brute force, but brute reason is quite unbearable. There is something unfair about its use. It is hitting below the intellect.

It is better to be beautiful than to be good, but it is better to be good than to be ugly.

The tragedy of old age is not that one is old, but that one is young.

The commonest thing is delightful if one only hides it.

The one charm of marriage is that it makes a life of deception necessary for both parties.

I can believe anything, provided it is incredible.

Good artists give everything to their art and consequently are perfectly uninteresting themselves.

When we think that we are experimenting on others, we are really experimenting on ourselves.

Those who are unfaithful know the pleasures of love; it is the faithful who know love's tragedies.

Never trust a woman who wears mauve or a woman over thirty-five who is fond of pink ribbons. It means they have a history.

It is personalities not principles that move the age.

No woman is a genius: women are a decorative sex. They never have anything to say, but they say it charmingly. They represent the triumph of matter over mind, just as men represent the triumph of mind over morals. There are only two kinds of women, the plain and the colored. The plain women are very useful. If you want to gain a reputation for respectability you have merely to take them down to supper. The other women are very charming. They commit one mistake, however. They paint in order to try to look young. Our grandmothers painted in order to try to talk brilliantly. Rouge and *esprit* used to go together. That has all gone out now. As long as a woman can look ten years younger than her own daughter she is perfectly satisfied.

If one hears bad music it is one's duty to drown it by one's conversation.

Only sentimentalists can repeat an emotion.

There is hardly a person in the House of Commons worth painting, though many of them would be better for a little whitewashing.

When one is in love one begins by deceiving oneself, one ends by deceiving others. That is what the world calls romance.

There is something infinitely mean about other people's tragedies.

Always! that is a dreadful word. Women are so fond of using it. They spoil every romance by trying to make it last forever.

Tea is the only simple pleasure left to us.

It is simply expression that gives reality to things.

The mind of a thoroughly well-informed man is like a bric-à-brac shop, all monsters and dust and everything priced above its proper value.

Phrases and Philosophies for the Use of the Young

THE FIRST duty in life is to be as artificial as possible. What the second duty is no one has yet discovered.

Wickedness is a myth invented by good people to account for the curious attractiveness of others.

Those who see any difference between soul and body have neither.

Religions die when they are proved to be true. Science is the record of dead religions.

The well bred contradict other people. The wise contradict themselves.

Nothing that actually occurs is of the smallest importance.

Dullness is the coming of age of seriousness.

If one tells the truth, one is sure, sooner or later, to be found out.

In all unimportant matters style not sincerity is the essential. In all important matters style not sincerity is the essential.

It is only by not paying our bills that we can hope to live in the memory of the commercial classes.

Only the shallow know themselves.

Time is waste of money.

There is a fatality about all good resolutions. They are invariably made too soon.

Any preoccupation with ideas of what is right or wrong in conduct shows an arrested intellectual development.

A truth ceases to be true when more than one person believes in it.

The vanishing point of social tolerance is represented by a woman without sentiment enough to yearn for love in a cottage, and without sense enough to refuse it.

Ambition is the last refuge of the failure.

One should either be a work of art, or wear a work of art.

It is only the superficial qualities that last. Man's deeper nature is soon found out.

Industry is the root of all ugliness.

The old believe everything; the middle aged suspect everything; the young know everything.

The condition of perfection is idleness; the aim of perfection is youth.

Modern morality consists in accepting the standard of one's age.

Women give to men the very gold of their lives, but they invariably want it back in very small change.

Some Oscariana

How fond women are of doing dangerous things. It is one of the qualities in them that I admire most.

A woman will flirt with anybody in the world as long as other people are looking on.

The costume of the nineteenth century is detestable. Sin is the only real color element left in modern life.

Evening clothes on a London merchant remind one of a morocco binding on a cook-book or a doily on a stove lid.

Credit is the capital of a younger son, and he can live charmingly on it.

To get back one's youth one has merely to repeat one's follies.

Nowadays most people die of a sort of creeping common sense, and discover, when it is too late, that the only things one never regrets are one's mistakes.

No civilized man ever regrets a pleasure, and no uncivilized man ever knows what a pleasure is.

The only horrible thing in the world is ennui. That is the one sin for which there is no forgiveness.

If a man treats life artistically, his brain is in his heart.

Most people become bankrupt through having invested too heavily in the prose of life. To have ruined oneself over poetry is an honor.

Being adored is a nuisance. Women treat us just as Humanity treats its gods. They worship us, and are always bothering us to do something for them.

Pleasure is nature's test, her sign of approval. When we are happy we are always good; but when we are good we are not always happy.

There is no such thing as an omen. Destiny does not send us heralds. She is too wise or too cruel for that.

A Radical is merely a man who has never dined, and a Tory simply a gentleman who has never thought.

The world has been made by fools that wise men may live in it.

FROM *The Decay of Lying*

IF A man is sufficiently unimaginative to produce evidence in support of a lie, he might just as well speak the truth at once.

Lying, the telling of beautiful untrue things, is the proper aim of Art.

Art reveals Nature's lack of design, her curious crudities, her absolutely unfinished condition. Nature has good intentions, but she cannot carry them out. Art is our gallant attempt to teach Nature her proper place.

The crude commercialism of America, its materializing spirit, its indifference to the poetical side of things, its lack of imagination and of high unattainable ideals, are entirely due to that country having adopted for its national hero one who, according to his own confession, was incapable of telling a lie; and it is not too much to say that the story of George Washington and the cherry tree has done more harm, and in a shorter space of time, than any other moral tale in the whole of literature.

The aim of the liar is simply to charm, to delight, to give pleasure. He is the very basis of civilized society.

Life imitates Art far more than Art imitates Life.

Literature always anticipates life. It does not copy it, but molds it to its purpose.

No great artist ever sees things as they really are. If he did, he would cease to be an artist.

Most of our modern portrait painters are doomed to absolute oblivion. They never paint what they see. They paint what the public sees, and the public never sees anything.

At twilight nature becomes a wonderfully suggestive effect, and is not without loveliness, though perhaps its chief use is to illustrate quotations from the poets.

We are a degraded race and have sold our birthright for a mess of facts.

People are beginning to be over-educated; at least everybody who is incapable of learning has taken to teaching.

Nature hates Mind. Thinking is the most unhealthy thing in the world, and people die of it just as they die of any other disease. Fortunately, in England at any rate, thought is not catching. Our splendid physique is entirely due to our national stupidity.

What is interesting about people in good society is the mask that each one of them wears, not the reality that lies behind the mask.

Many a young man starts in life with a natural gift of exaggeration which, if nurtured in congenial and sympathetic surroundings, might grow into something really great and wonderful. But, as a rule, he comes to nothing. He either falls into careless habits of accuracy, or takes to frequenting the society of the aged and well-informed. Both things are equally fatal to his imagination, as indeed they would be fatal to the imagination of anybody, and in a short time he develops a morbid and unhealthy faculty of truth telling, begins to verify all statements made in his presence, has no hesitation in contradicting people who are much younger than himself, and often ends by writing novels which are so like life that no one can possibly believe in their probability.

It is immoral to use private property in order to alleviate the horrible evils that result from the institution of private property.

Lying for the sake of the improvement of the young, which is the basis of home education, still lingers among us, but the only form of lying that is absolutely beyond reproach is lying for its own sake, and the highest development of this is, lying in art.

One touch of Nature may make the whole world kin, but two touches of Nature will destroy any work of art.

The only beautiful things are the things that do not concern us.

Nobody of any real culture ever talks nowadays about the beauty of the sunset. Sunsets are quite old-fashioned.

There are three kinds of despots. There is the despot who tyrannizes over the body. There is the despot who tyrannizes over the soul. There is the despot who tyrannizes over the soul and body alike. The first is called the Prince. The second is called the Pope. The third is called the People.

Evolution is the law of life, and there is no evolution save toward Individualism.

All bad art comes from returning to Life and Nature and elevating them into ideals. Life and Nature may sometimes be used as part of Art's rough material, but before they are of any real service to Art they must be translated into artistic conventions.

Nature is always behind the age.

FROM *The Critic as Artist*

A LITTLE sincerity is a dangerous thing. All bad poetry springs from genuine feeling. To be natural is to be obvious, and to be obvious is to be inartistic.

I dislike modern memoirs. They are generally written by people who have either entirely lost their memories, or have never done anything worth remembering; which, however, is, no doubt, the true explanation of their popularity, as the English public always feels perfectly at its ease when a mediocrity is talking to it.

The public is wonderfully tolerant. It forgives everything except genius.

Every great man nowadays has his disciples, and it is always Judas who writes the biography.

Learned conversation is either the affectation of the ignorant or the profession of the mentally unemployed.

Truth, in matters of religion, is simply the opinion that has survived.

Man is a rational animal who always loses his temper when he is called upon to act in accordance with the dictates of reason.

Just as the philanthropist is the nuisance of the ethical sphere, so the nuisance of the intellectual sphere is the man who is so occupied in trying to educate others, that he has never had any time to educate himself.

It is only an auctioneer who can equally and impartially admire all schools of art.

There are two ways of disliking art. One is to dislike it. The other is to like it rationally.

We live in the age of the over-worked, and the under-educated; the age in which people are so industrious that they become absolutely stupid.

How appalling is the ignorance which is the inevitable result of the fatal habit of imparting opinions!

There is only one thing worse than Injustice, and that is Justice without her sword in her hand. When Right is not Might, it is Evil.

England has done one thing; it has invented and established public opinion, which is an attempt to organize the ignorance of the community, and to elevate it to the dignity of physical force.

When man acts he is a puppet. When he describes he is a poet.

To be good according to the vulgar standard of goodness is quite easy. It merely requires a certain amount of sordid terror, a certain lack of imaginative thought, and a certain low passion for middle-class respectability.

The basis of action is lack of imagination. It is the last resource of those who know not how to dream.

Modern journalism justifies its own existence by the great Darwinian principle of the survival of the vulgarest.

Conversation should touch everything, but should concentrate itself on nothing.

Those who try to lead the people can only do so by following the mob.

The mere existence of conscience is a sign of our imperfect development. It must be merged in instinct before we become fine. Self-denial is simply a method by which man arrests his progress.

The difference between literature and journalism is that journalism is unreadable, and literature is not read.

There is much to be said in favor of modern journalism. By giving us the opinions of the uneducated, it keeps us in touch with the ignorance of the community.

As for begging, it is safer to beg than to take, but it is finer to take than to beg.

Science is out of the reach of morals, for her eyes are fixed upon eternal truths. Art is out of the reach of morals, for her eyes are fixed upon things beautiful and immortal and ever-changing.

Though of all poses a moral pose is the most offensive, still to have a pose at all is something. It is a form of recognition of the importance of treating life from a definite and reasoned standpoint.

Life makes us pay too high a price for its wares, and we purchase the meanest of its secrets at a cost that is monstrous and infinite.

It takes a thoroughly selfish age, like our own, to deify self-sacrifice.

Indiscretion is the better part of valor. The sure way of knowing nothing about life is to try to make oneself useful.

The basis of action is lack of imagination. It is the last resource of those who know not how to dream.

Cheap editions of great books may be delightful, but cheap editions of great men are absolutely detestable.